Scrapes and Scars

No Secrets

Scrapes and Scars

No Secrets

Scrapes and Scars: No Secrets

Chavonne Hurdle

LET'S NOT FORGET, LLC

PHILADELPHIA

SCRAPES AND SCARS: NO SECRETS

Let's Not Forget, LLC / Prodigy Gold Books

Let's Not Forget, LLC E-book edition/June 2018

Let's Not Forget, LLC Paperback edition/June 2018

Copyright (c) 2018 by Chavonne Hurdle

Library of Congress Catalog Card Number: 2018938691

Website: http://www.cbhurdle.com

Author's e-mail: Chavonne.hurdle@gmail.com

While the author has taken utmost efforts to ensure the accuracy of the written content, all readers are advised to follow information mentioned herein at their own risk. The author and publisher cannot be held responsible for any personal or commercial damage caused by misinterpretation of any information present in this book. All readers are encouraged to seek professional advice as and when needed.

All rights reserved. No parts of this book may be used or reproduced in any manner whatsoever without written permission from the author, except in case of brief quotations embodied in critical articles and reviews.

ISBN 978-1-939665-69-0

Published simultaneously in the US and Canada

PRINTED IN THE UNITED STATES OF AMERICA

Dedication

Writing this book gives me the avenue of sharing with thousands of young and adult women all over the world, who to this day, continue to hold their story a secret because they are afraid of who it might hurt.

I'm here to tell you this: "You are not alone anymore" and "You are no longer a prisoner of your own thoughts or a victim, but a survivor and survivors live on, if not for any other reason than simply to tell their (our) story."

You (us) no longer have to live and suffer in silence anymore. Let's speak out so that it can help us live and be better women, and importantly to become better mothers.

I want to let you in on a little secret; our parents, family members and even the offender will continue to live their life to the best of their abilities knowing your secret and what they did or didn't do to help you. Sadly, this is how life works. I am attempting to enjoy the fruits of life just like them, but I cannot do it unless I set myself free of all these secrets, you should try to do the same.

"Not under the power or control of another but free and able to act or be done as one may desires."

At first, it may seem hard but once you put one foot in front of the other and start believing in yourself again there will be small holes that will begin to let light shine in your dark tunnel. Before you know it, there will be so much light that you will need sunglasses because the light will begin to hurt your eyes.

Trust the process…

Acknowledgement

I thank God for his endless love and his consistent blessings in my life. I thank God for embracing me with the ability to overcome the obstacles that I have faced and providing me the courage to accept those who offered their help and assistance. You are truly a savior. Thank you, Lord.

My husband, Joel, from day one you have remained truly a great man. With the fine lines of my situations and the depths of my secrets that I have shared with you, I could only expect you to vanish out of my life, yet you remained solid as a rock but warm enough for me to lean on and take comfort from your presence. I love you.

Taking the role of a mother has been a great challenge and has been the greatest gift of my life. To my kids; Amirah, Lavonne, Alejah, Joel Jr. and Enrique Jr. I am so proud to be your mother. When I cried, you guys make me smile. Just when I wanted to give up in life, you guys gave me a reason to continue striving. Just when I felt that there was no hope, you gave me a reason to get right back up and fight. You all have shown me what it means to be a mother and have made me realize what life is all about.

We laughed, we cried, we fussed, and fought, yet we always found a way to come together and unite as a family once again. Because of you guys, I will forever continue to strive for the best and aim for success. You all will continue to magically shine and be that light of my guidance. Mama loves you.

Last but not least, I would like to take the time to

specially thank my mentors in no particular order, Dr. P. McPherson-Myers, Dr. M. Davis and A. Robinson. It's tough for an African American woman to be surrounded by positive individuals like yourselves.

I consider myself blessed to be surrounded and be guided by you all! You have inspired me to be motivated, enthusiastic and to aggressively approach my dreams.

I love you all.

Foreword

In a 2012 survey on National Intimate Partner and Sexual Violence by the Center for Disease Control, it was found that approximately 8% or an estimated 10 million girls under the age of 18 experienced rape or attempted rape. The study also found that among the female victims under the age of 18 who experienced sexual violence, 43.6% of the completed or attempted rape was committed by an acquaintance, and 27.7% by a family member.[1]

All too often we hear about the tragic end result of sexual violence, and psychological, emotional, and physical abuse, but rarely do we understand the depth of the pain, guilt, and resilience of the survivors. Until now…in *Scrapes and Scars*, Chavonne Hurdle shares her deepest, personal experiences and memories in hopes of helping with the healing process of those who have had similar experiences or those who are currently in similar circumstances, as well as to help others who may be in relationship with abused women better understand the challenges faced when childhood and adult trauma exist.

I met Chavonne when I was a college counselor- a young lady, right out of high school, Chavonne was eager to begin her college career and determined to succeed. A tough exterior, but a soft, beautiful smile and charming personality to match, she was strong, focused and determined to be the first in her family to obtain a college degree. During our weekly meetings we laughed and chatted about her social life and her friends, college experiences, and employment opportunities – never did I suspect that she had been through the turmoil and trauma described in this book, and never could I have predicted the challenges that await her.. But as

---

[1] https://www.cdc.gov/violenceprevention/sexualviolence/index.html

time progressed, and layers unfolded, our relationship developed and my admiration for her grew.

Almost 20 years ago I met a young lady full of dreams, but little did I know, equally full of pain. Over the years I witnessed Chavonne find her inner strength and a way out of no way. Strong beyond measure, she never complained.. to look at her you never saw signs of the chaos she was dealing with.. a master of wearing masks, she somehow managed to compartmentalize her pain and continue functioning with excellence- in work and in school. As I reflect on our conversations, she would share some of the dysfunction she was dealing with through her sense of humor, making jokes to lighten the heaviness of the situations, which gave the impression that she is "ok". I later realized all of this was more of a coping mechanism.

As time went on and she began to share more intimate details of her life, the numerous accounts of betrayal, mistrust and hurt by the very people who were supposed to love and protect her. I admired her ability to be vulnerable and to ask for help, advice, and guidance when she knew the burden was becoming too much to bear. I recognized a shift in Chavonne when she was in her lowest moments, when she realized she could not handle any more on her own, and would no longer wrap her pain in jokes, but she started to openly share her awareness of her own behaviors that were detrimental to her well-being. I recognized that it was her way of asking for help.

Although I worried about Chavonne, I was never worried *for* Chavonne. At her most difficult times, she held on to her internal belief that there was more for her to accomplish, more for her to learn, more for her to do, that giving up was not an option, and happiness was obtainable.

With all that she has endured, it has not hardened her or decreased her capacity to love unconditionally or dim her sense of humor. She still uses humor to laugh at how unbelievably crazy life can be, but now, she is aware of how to protect herself from people who are toxic and unable or unwilling to love her the way she deserves to be loved.

Her drive to be healthy and happy is unmatched. Every time I talk to her she has researched new information to open up home for homeless girls, completed another degree (with honors), certificate or licensure, or was promoted. There isn't a job she has applied for that she hasn't received an offer. She strives for excellence and her self-discipline has helped her remain focused through the years. I continue to be amazed as I have watched her grow into this beautiful mother, wife, daughter, friend. She is selfless, kind, generous and compassionate.

This book is the capstone of her healing. Although therapeutic for her, it is also a continuation of her passion and legacy to help some others. As you read through her pain from childhood through adulthood, you will recognize a common theme of resilience and strength.

Although I wish this were not her story, I believe she was called to heal others. I continue to be amazed, in awe and proud of the Chavonne Hurdle.

—**Penny McPherson-Myers, Ed.D**

Opening Statement

The worst thing about sexual, emotional, physical, and psychological abuse is you never know when you will have flashbacks. These old vivid memories come at uncertain times and can be brought on by certain touches, smells, and songs that have the potential to send me into an anxiety attack. For instance, I can't listen to Frankie Beverly and Maze's Song, *Happy Feeling*.

When I hear that song it makes my heart turn cold. My heart beats faster then my breath can catch up. You see, that is the song he used to always play and sing. When I hear that song it makes me think of how and when I wanted to kill Chester slowly. How I wanted to torture him to death. To listen to his screams as I used to hear my own as he ravished and destroyed me. The smell of brut or old spice cologne turns my stomach upside down and makes me want to puke. Only then, did I want to do myself in.

As a young child in my home, certain topics were not talked about because of the fear of the power of knowledge. Topics like sex, drugs, education, and relationships were off limits. Some children were raised on morals and values, that said, "Children are to be seen and not heard." That's how my household was run. Growing up I heard my parents say, "What you do in the dark, will come to light." My personal favorite was, "What goes on in our house, stays in our house." I hate that saying to this day.

Who made that up?

Whoever it was deserved an ass kicking because parents

used such sayings to hide the dirty secrets in their homes. This saying allows children to get hurt. Some children are so scared that if they tell anything, their parents would be angry with them and forced young children to believe that if they did tell things, some adults would be in trouble. The fact that they deserved trouble was of no ones concern.

I suffered terribly due to that phase in particular. I wondered if my deep, dark, and terrible secret was finally revealed, who would believe me? Who would it hurt? Would everyone be upset with me if I severely disrupted the family unit?

To hell with everyone else. What about me? Who really cares about me? Would anyone come to my rescue if they knew he what he was doing to me. Would they come with open arms holding and rocking me to sleep if they knew? I lived with selfish thoughts because of my hurting. Healing, I had no desire to do so for many of years. I wanted everyone to hurt like me. But, even as I acted tough, I had a conscious that played on my mind telling me I wasn't who I was pretending to be. When I hurt people I beat myself up and wanted to run to them and apologize. My pride wouldn't let me do it.

So, I went through childhood without any hopes. My dreams were snatched away. I was misguided and lost. I found myself escaping the wiles of childhood trauma for the traumas of adulthood. It wasn't until I trusted someone with my secret who in turn, referred me to a counselor, and that's when the healing process started. .

The pivotal part of healing for me was understanding

that what happened was *not* my fault. It is never the victim's fault, regardless of how they may be stigmatized by a calloused and uncaring, society. Reliving your truth can be painful, but it is freeing.

Sadly, it will always be a part of my life's history. However, it does not and will not continue to control my life.

Not anymore.

My motivation is knowing that my story is your story. And I refuse to hold this poison in my system any longer. I will tell our story. My hopes through your reading of this book is you will learn how family secrets can destroy your heart, to bring awareness, and start the conversation. Being raped, molested and sexually abused is the worse crime imaginable and can ultimately change who you are but, there is life, after. A good one.

"It's not what happens to you, but how you react to it that matters."—Epictetus

Table of Contents

Chapter 1	1	Retrospection
Chapter 2	6	The Unexpected "P"
Chapter 3	12	I Thought My Dad Knew
Chapter 4	22	Unstable "Help"
Chapter 5	26	Letters to My Parents
Chapter 6	29	Self-harm
Chapter 7	32	Freshman Year
Chapter 8	41	It Got Worse Before…
Chapter 9	48	Graduation Day
Chapter 10	70	When It Became Real…
Chapter 11	75	Stranded
Chapter 12	80	Rock Bottom
Chapter 13	86	Rewind
Chapter 14	89	Lasting Effects
A Final Note	93	
12-Day Journal	97	

Scrapes and Scars

No Secrets

1
Restrospection

I was the fourth of five biological children and my parents adopted six foster children. I have a twin brother Edward who was born a minute before me. Let him tell it, he drags it out to about five minutes. We were born prematurely. I was one pound and Edward was two pounds. We lived in an incubator for a few months. Edward left before me because I struggled to gain weight. My mother smoked cigarettes and was sick a lot during her pregnancy. Maybe that's why I stay sick so much today.

Growing up our home was the party house. That's what I called it. My parents had parties or hosted them and everyone in the family and their friends came over and had a good time. As I got older, I started to see that our home was open to whomever, whenever. If my older brother's friends didn't have a place to live, they came to stay at our house. If family members got kicked out their house, they came to stay with us, too. It didn't matter, our home was where everyone ran.

My parents were cool to everyone but their own children or maybe just me. It was more mother than my father. My relationship with them changed as I got older. They were strict. My mother was a stay at home parent so some working parents in our neighborhood hired her to babysit their children. It was never quiet in our home. My father worked second shift for a mailing equipment company. All my father ever wanted was a clean house. Oh and alcohol. No matter what time he came home from work—or the bar—at 1:00 or 2:00 in the morning, if his house wasn't clean he woke up everyone. He didn't care if we had school in the morning. We had to rise and clean to his liking. It was embarrassing when friends slept over and my dad came home drunk, yelling at us to clean the house, and he would speak in other languages that everyone got a good laugh out of. To this day, we're not sure what language he spoke when he was drunk. Even though, I hated it as a child I love that about my dad. My obsession for cleaning is because of him.

My mother, on the other, was the disciplinarian. If you

did anything wrong, you deserved a whipping. She was the judge and the jury in the house. Whatever she said goes. Period. If we didn't follow the rules there were real consequences. I hardly ever saw her smile. She never played with us. I only have one memory with her that I will always cherish. She signed me up for Girl Scouts. At the time, I had to be about nine- or ten-years-old. I entered as a junior girl scout. I wore that green uniform with pride. The joy of being a part of something excited me.

This one event we participated in was the 5k Walk or Run in Philadelphia. We had spent that day walking with other girls and their mothers in the Logan section of Philadelphia. The smile on my face as I looked out at everyone and up at my mother was priceless. I felt like I finally made a connection with her like the girls did on TV and movies with their mom. I thought I was about to embark on a mother and daughter relationship that was out this world. That day, I thought we had built a great bond and I was excited about spending more time with her, since a lot of her time went to helping and babysitting other people's children. Shortly after that event, I don't remember anything else we did together. I even stopped going to Girl Scouts.

In middle school, I was a tomboy. All I wore was baggy clothes, played video games, and enjoyed sports. Edward and I created a dance group and we were in singing group with our friends in the neighborhood. But my favorite things were basketball, reading, and dancing. Edward and I went around Philly during the summer, attending block parties and challenging other kids in the community to dance contests. My older brother, Derrick, was our manager. He was five-years-older than us. He taught us new dance steps, or we watched videos of music groups like, Kid-n-Play, and used their moves. We never lost a competition. The thrill of going to other neighborhoods and having strangers watch us perform was incredible. It gave me a rush. Back then, I felt like me and Edward were destined to be stars. To be great. We were the totally package.

Being a twin was fun and we made it fun like we were identical twins. One time in school we switched classes and sat at each other desk as if the teachers wouldn't figure out we didn't belong there during roll call. Edward and I were jokesters. It was nice making people smile and laugh. We always had a good time everywhere we went. Derrick was funny, too. He taught me a lot of things. He even had me in the corner store hustling his friends for money, playing them in arcade games like Street Fighter and Mortal Combat. I played on the game all day with one quarter. We even hookied school one day playing on the video game. It wasn't our intention we just lost track of time.

The older I got the more obsessed I became with

anything that I had the opportunity to learn something new. I wouldn't stop it until I mastered it. Derrick even taught me how to fight. I had an in-home punching bag: Edward. For years, Derrick made us fight and he would watch. All the times when we fought, I would beat up Edward, until one day he must had hit puberty because he was losing, and all of a sudden, he picked me up, slammed me down and I was out. That was the last time me and Edward fought each other. All my memories before twelve-years-old were fun-filled. I was finding myself until Chester showed up, and then, my life took a turn for the worse.

2

The Unexpected "P"

As a kid I was never shocked that someone was coming to stay with us for whatever reason. Seeing my parents always willing to help anyone out, taught me how to be a giver, and not a taker. However, at the age of twelve, that changed. One day, I overheard my mother on the phone, telling someone how Chester had started drinking a lot, and had started using drugs. Perhaps, that was why his wife did not want to deal with him any longer, my mom had said. She informed the caller, he could come and stay with her until he got on his feet.

When Chester usually came to visit, he always presented himself as laid-back and super cool. He always made jokes and was the life of the party. Generally, he was OK to be around when he did come by the house. But this time when he came to live with us, he came as an entirely different person.

My memory is a little fuzzy here, or perhaps my young and immature mind purposely locked away the initial memories, so that they couldn't hurt me again. I am not quite sure how long after he moved in that he started sexually assaulting me.

One weekend his children—yes, he actually had those—came to visit and he went out for a while. Being the oldest in the house during this time, I made sure to keep them from getting bored so we played and played until we fell asleep that night in the basement in Chester's bed with my parents upstairs.

While asleep, I felt something heavy lying on me. A strong smell of smoke, cologne, and alcohol pouring off someone that made my nose itch, forcing me to wake up. As I rubbed my eyes with my hands, I was trying to remove what was on top of me, but he refused to let me up no matter how much I tried to push.

"No, please stop." I cried as he continued to force himself on me.

"Shut up. You're going to wake up the kids. Shut up.

Shut up," he kept saying in an aggressive tone. I quietly cried in fear because I didn't want to wake the kids lying on the bed beside us. I told Chester to stop, again. I pleaded in all the ways my twelve year old mind knew how.

He just kept telling me to shut up.

I tried to bite his hand that was covering my mouth, so he squeezed my cheeks together so hard I thought one of my teeth had actually fallen out when he let go.

Then he said, "If you tell, no one would believe you."

I feared that this was a fact. He was my mother's relative. Who would believe me if I told, he had feasted on my innocence? He did it right beside his own children at night with my parents in the house.

I weighed my options. He was already having his way with me. My struggles to fight Chester off seemed to ignite his excitement. I gave up fighting. I was no match for him. I laid there like a limp and broken rag doll. As tears came down my face all I thought about was how no one would believe me. What may have only been but a few minutes seemed to stretch for a never-ending eternity.

I felt alone, so alone I thought I only had to fight for myself. I believed his words when he said no one would believe me because my mother would believe his lie. She had stressed, in the past, how family business should always remain within the house.

My eyes were closed as he finally found my opening and pushed. Ripping though my flesh, I closed my eyes tighter, clench my teeth together and balled my fist up to maybe control some of the pain as he pounded and pounded away at my vagina whispering to me all the time, "*Vonnie, damn you are a special girl.*"

When he let me up, I looked at him from the middle of the stairs in disbelief. I tiptoed upstairs to the bathroom to wash my skin, and to scrub his filth off my body. As I wiped my own vagina it burned so bad that I almost hit my face on the sink due to the pain weakening my legs. My legs felt like rubber bands. In my head, I kept replaying his voice telling me to shut up. Then seeing the blood on my rag made me cry harder. His brutal assault had torn through my sensitive opening badly enough to make me bleed.

That night, I was forced to lie in bed with a rag between my legs because I did not want the blood coming out of me to leave its mark on the sheets. Blood on the sheets would lead to questions and questions meant I had to provide answers. This wouldn't be answering mere questions. Even as a child I knew that I did not have the strength to give answers to defiling questions. How would I explain to anyone? What if no one believed me? Plus, the water was warm and it eased some of the throbbing I had down there. The rag between my legs felt like the only safe way out for the night. I decided I could not afford to let anyone see the evidence of my violation. Not on my bed. Not where anyone else could see my shame. The next day, I planned to be the first out of bed to dispose of the rag.

Disoriented: "To confuse by removing or obscuring something that has guided a person, group, or culture, as customs, and moral standard."

Everything that I knew was taken from me that night and I had no idea how to go back. When someone touched me I was jumpy. I could sit and just fall into a daze. It hurt when I walked. For many days, it felt like my vagina was on fire. It hurt when I peed and every time I whipped myself I looked at the rag or tissue to see if I was still bleeding.

Why me? This question haunted me every day. I laid in my bed the first time it happened thinking and asking God, why me? What have I done so wrong that I deserve this to happen to me?

At twelve-years-old, no child should have felt that kind of pain. I blamed myself for what happened. I blamed myself for being with his children and for falling asleep in his bed.

SCRAPES & SCARS

I blamed myself for fighting and saying no. Maybe the pain wouldn't have been so bad if I didn't fight him. The word *no* did not mean anything to me anymore. I said, "no" so many times. He never listened so I simply went ahead and removed the word from my vocabulary.

3

I Thought My Dad Knew

"I cannot think of any need in childhood as strong as the need for a father's protection."—Sigmund Freud

As I slept in bed, I was suddenly awakened in the middle of the night by a finger in my vagina, a hand over my mouth, and the nasty smell of cigarettes. When I opened my eyes, Chester was gazing right into my eyes, as if he was trying to look for some kind of connection with me. I quickly closed them tightly shut and held them closed for as long as I could. My heart was beating fast out of my chest. He climbed into bed with me, I balled my fist up, clenched my teeth as he violated my body again.

SCRAPES & SCARS

All of a sudden, I heard a fire alarm screaming. Before he climaxed, he quickly jumped off the bed, fixing his clothes. My father walked into my room and asked, "Are you cooking something on the stove? It's burning."

Chester said, "Yes," and simply walked out of my room.

I lay there waiting and trying to hear my father's voice. But I heard nothing. Then, I heard the door closing to my parent's bedroom. Sitting up in bed, I was amazed that he never asked Chester, 'Why the hell are you in my daughter's bedroom at this time of night?' Never did I hear those words from my father. Why? Did he not just see what happened? He was in here and I'm not imaging this, he just left. To me I begin to think that I was a sacrifice or a debt my parent's couldn't pay. I lay on my bed crying with my face in my hand hurting, thinking; *can these people really not care about me?* Is he that naïve? What did I do to my dad for him to ignore me this way?

The thought of dying ran through my mind and I needed to find away to do it.

Suicide.

I had heard about a girl in my middle school that tried it. But did I really want to die or just draw enough attention to myself so that my parents could see that something was not right with me.

> "Smile, because it confuses people. Smile, because it's easier than explaining what is killing you inside."—
> **Anonymous**

Smiling was something I knew how to do without prompts. It became so easy to hide my hurt because there was never a follow-up question when people saw you smiling. I had become a master of disguise.

Smiling gave people the sense that I was approachable; my face said I was, but my heart was cold. As far as I was concerned, smiling was a conduit that gave people the impression that I was that oh-such-a-sweet-and-nice-girl, whilst I had this fire and rage smoldering deep inside of me. If anyone ever dared to say anything wrong to me, I chewed them up like there was no tomorrow.

But I had no idea how to stand up against Chester. I was this tough mean girl to others but could not fight him off. I was so angry with myself for not being strong enough to deal with him like everyone else. Then, the angry, defiant, anti-social girl came out. I got into fights at school and around the neighborhood. I disrespected authority figures and hated everyone. While in school, I walked with my head down because I was afraid that teachers and staff would see what was behind my eyes. So I kept smiling. That drew many teachers and staff closer to me but I never let them in.

Despite all of that, I had an outlet.

Basketball.

Books.

My passion and love for basketball kept me sane and was the sole silver lining on an otherwise incredibly dark cloud. It was my ticket to freedom. Reading not so much, I stopped reading because when it was quiet it allowed my mind to drift off and it became hard to focus on the words. Instead, I relived what Chester was doing to me. It played in my mind like a the rerun of a movie.

I barely was making my grades at school and was firmly convinced that there would come a day in my life when I would play professional basketball. There were talks that there would be a WNBA soon and my game was getting better everyday. I walked everyday to the basketball courts in Nicetown, but one day there was a portable court on the corner of my street in Philadelphia. Not a crate but a real court. I'm not sure who basketball court it was, but it was always there and everyone around the way came to play on it. On that court was where my game elevated with the help of Brian and a few other guys.

Brian was a friend of Derrick's. He was six-years-older

than me, out of high school. and working on becoming a nurse. Brian was a typical boy next door—charming, popular, and well respected. No one suspected that he indulged in a life of smoking, drinking, and partying. He had a great personality and a smile that all the girls loved. He was a ladies man that wanted all of the girls. And he never hid it.

I had a crush on Brian. He didn't mind that I was younger than he was. He lived across the street from us and he enjoyed playing basketball too. We clicked immediately as friends first. He taught me the mental toughness and emotional piece of the game. We played rough-house together all the time and he never took it easy on me. *Oh, I'm girl talk,* didn't work on him. He was determined to help me be great. We played on teams together and won a few games for money. Basketball was my way out of this. Little did I realize, basketball would provide Chester the opportunity he needed!

One hot, dreadful day, I was playing basketball at Hunting Park near my grandmother's home. When I was done playing, I realized that I had lost all track of time. My heart sank. In a panic I ran with weak legs to my grandma's house and called my mom to let her know that I was about to start walking home. She insisted that I wait for Chester to come pick me up because it was dark. I took the phone from my ear and looked at it, as I didn't want to hear those words come out her mouth.

There was so much I wanted to tell her, so much I wanted to say, how *he* was the person, with whom I was not allowed to walk home alone, in the dark. The living embodiment of every parent's nightmare I lived in, but…I said nothing. With hesitation, my breath was caught in my throat and my voice was gone. I could only mumble a semi-coherent, "OK" and hung up.

As I began that long walk home, my heart beat fast, eye rolling back and forth, and my mind pacing on which way to go. It felt as if I was walking to my execution. Perhaps, that was precisely what it was. I felt as if I was walking in a nightmare as I concentrated on taking one step at a time. I was walking with the speed of an inchworm. My stomach clenched into a thousand little knots as I thought with dread what was surely about to happen.

I thought I could avoid him seeing me by walking through the park, thinking that he would look for me on the regular route. Boy was I wrong. I did not have to walk far before his hated voice rang out, "*Vonnie get in.*"

My worst fear had come true. He had found me.

I tried to pretend that I had not heard him by ignoring his increasingly persistent calls even as he drove slower to make sure that I had heard and saw him. People had started to take notice by then, and I did not want to draw any more attention to myself. I resigned to the inevitable and got into the van, even though deep inside, I was screaming to just get out and run. Run for my life and never stop. But I was afraid to. Afraid of Chester catching me and doing unspeakable things as punishment. As if this wasn't punishment enough. I was a scared and a lonely little girl who had no one to turn to, so I kept quiet.

I sat there like a mannequin in the back seat as he commenced driving around in circles all over the park. Eventually, he slowed his van down and gave me an order to come and sit up front with him. Sitting there with my head in my hand and heart beating fast, I was barely able to catch my breath. I felt like a fish out of water. Chester called my name at least fifty more times and that last time he called me, I could hear the barely concealed rage in his voice. Oh, I knew that tone so well. He used it only when he wanted to intentionally hurt me. With total resistance, I sat in the front passenger seat and he immediately put his hand on my young scaly thigh.

He drove around with his hand firmly placed on my lap trying to find the right place to park. We are never going home I kept thinking. I tried futilely to pry his huge fingers from my lap, but I failed to do so. In fact, that only made it worse.

SCRAPES & SCARS

I continued to move his hand. He placed it back on my lap with more force and strength as he continued to reach for my vagina. He slowly pulled into a parking spot and I immediately began to have a panic attack. My heart was throbbing violently—hard and fast—I think if anyone stood right in front of me they could see my heart in a race, running where my feet could not carry me. My eyes became hazy and lost their focus since I was not able to see anything except blurred images. I was not aware of it, but I was hyperventilating.

I couldn't look at anything but the streetlights that beamed down over his blue van. As he quickly got out of his seat he unbuckled his belt, took down his pants and started touching himself. His movements were fluid and measured with practiced ease as if he did this sort of thing on a regular basis. He grabbed my hand and pulled me from my seat all the way to the back of the van in one smooth motion.

I remember the spot where he parked the van today. This was the spot where the sex workers stood and auctioned off their services to work. That was the reason why no one gave a damn whoever was there getting fucked.

He flung himself down on me and as usual my pleas of *please, stop,* and *no* were ignored. Even as he forced my clothes down, he kept muttering the same hypocritical phrase, "*Vonnie you are special.*" With clenched teeth and balled fist I lost the strength to resist and he perpetuated on me the greatest indignity that a man can on a little girl.

With every word, every cry, it seemed like his pumps or strokes got harder and harder as if he was getting off not so much on the sexual nature of the rape, but the fact that he was hurting me so much. My pitiful attempts at protecting myself served only to arouse Chester more. He was like a vile beast slobbering over its feast.

The more I cried the harder he pounded into me. My tears continued to flow to the point where I believe I passed out from the agony. *A kid is supposed to be cared for, you sick son of a bitch. If I had a gun, I would kill you right where you stand. You bloody bastard.*

I woke up, I was fully dressed, and Chester was ordering me to get out of the van because we were home. Then, he whispered his final admonition, secure in the sure knowledge that it would seal my lips completely, "You better not say a word or your mother will lose her foster kids."

As I slowly trudged up the stairs into the house with my head down in shame, all I thought about was with all of the adult women walking around the neighborhood, why the hell do you want to fuck a little girl?

I immediately went into the bathroom and cried a river as I tried to scrub the nasty odor of his sweat off my skin.

SCRAPES & SCARS

The harder I scrubbed, the more his scent stayed on me. I felt his disgusting breath on my face. The foul stench of Chester permeated the marrow of my bones.

4

Unstable "Help"

"Your emotions are very unstable and should never be the foundation for direction for your life"—Joyce Meyer

A cloud of shame held over my head every single day and it weighed heavy on me. Chester was doing many sexual things to me and I had no idea why my body was turning on me the way that it did. I was even embarrassed because Chester would say things like, "I know you like it because your getting wet, your body is responding to me." I did not want Chester to do those things to me at all. My mind was playing so many tricks on me and I wanted it all to stop. But didn't know how.

SCRAPES & SCARS

My childhood was gloom as a result of the repeated attacks. At that young age, the whole world was closing in on me and I did not want to live with the pain anymore. Thoughts of dying came more frequent and it gave me the modicum of solace I craved.

I had a reason for thinking like this; I was going through something I didn't know how to deal with, nor who to tell about it. The cards were stacked against me and I was ready to burn them down.

My first suicide attempt came the day my beloved uncle June bug died. I was thirteen. He died in the middle room of our house. My mother wanted to help take care of him before he passed. As I was sat on the floor by my bed crying, Chester came into my room, and attempted to console me. He kneeled down on one knee and started rubbing my back and saying it was all right. As I continued to shrug and move away from his touches, he moved in the same direction as me, then, he grabbed me by my wrist and pulled me close to him. He stood up and pulled me closer. He inhaled the scent of my hair while attempted to pull my pants down.

I was too stunned to even realize what he was doing. But knew it was a useless struggle again. I remember the searing pain as he tore me apart when he entered me, raping me, while there had just been a dead body in the other room. He blocked the doorway by standing there so no one was able to come in. While standing, he had his hand over my mouth and he inserted himself inside of me. But it wasn't working well for him so he turned me around, slightly bent me over and inserted himself inside me again and with every new stroke I tried to find something in the room to stare at until it was over but I couldn't. I kept having visions of somebody breaking down the door to come and save me from Chester, but no one came to rescue me.

No one

Not then, not ever.

After he was done, he casually handed me whatever dirty garment was on the floor and told me to wipe myself. Then, he kissed me and told me I was special, and left my room.

I fell to the floor and curled into the fetal position, cried with my head in my hands, and rocked my body. My dad came in soon after to check on me but he thought I was crying for my uncle June Bug and told me everything would be all right. In my head, I told dad, "You are so fucking late. Where were you just two minutes ago? Damn you!" Little did dad know, I would never ever be all right. I was never going to be OK. And it would take much more than unknowing reassurance to soothe my inner ache.

Later that night, I went into my father's bathroom

cabinet and took a handful of ibuprofen and Tylenol. Afterward, I went into my uncle June Bug's room, and took some of the AIDS pills he had left over. I quickly ran into the bathroom—with no hesitation—turned the tap water on, tossed the pills in my mouth, put my hands under the facet and took a few great gulps of water. I then went into my room, laid down in bed to write my parents a suicide note, and talked to God about how sorry I was for ending my life so soon.

    I dozed off.

5

Letters to My Parents

"When I'm dead maybe then, you would realize just how much hurt and pain I suffered from."—Chavonne Hurdle

To my Mother:

Dear mom,

    I can never understand how someone could be a housewife but never do anything with their children at home. How did you allow things to happen in your house when you were always there? You never looked at me or came looking for me. I needed you to come find me and you never did. Didn't my walk or talk change? Didn't you hear me calling out to you in silence? I prayed for you to feel my spirit being broken and my body being violated but you never came. I needed you more than you will ever know or understand.

Why did you hate me so much?

What did I do so wrong?

I felt your hate towards me just by the way you looked at me. My death is your fault.

Goodbye!

"Love and fear, everything the father of a family says must inspire one or the other"—Joseph J'ouvert

To my Father:

Dear Dad,

Some of my best memories are with you. I was so happy when you came to one of my basketball games. The feeling of looking out and seeing your face walk through those doors brightened up my day and my heart. I wanted to shed tears of joy. I am forever grateful to have felt that support from you.

I remember you would take me to the dentist. I never understood why you had to take me after working all night and mom always stayed home and babysat other people's children. There were times when you took us to our favorite pizza spot "Kings Pizza" on Saturdays when we went food shopping. I wanted to tell you so much. But right after you ordered our pizza you took yourself off to the liquor bar. I always wanted to ask you how you could absorb yourself in your work and alcohol so much. Why did you trust her to *raise us even when she let you do the job of bringing us up while she raised her own boys? Boys she doted on, but who had nothing to do with you at times.*

It always felt so strange to me that you never suspected anything. As my father, you provided for the family financially however, you forgot the main component and that's to provide protection for your kids. So, my death is also your fault.

Goodbye

6

Self-harm

Sunlight beamed through my semi-closed curtains and the sound of people talking outside of my window streamed inside. I couldn't believe what had happened. Why am I awake? Shouldn't I be dead? I asked myself. Did I not take the pills correctly? I lay in bed, banging my head on my pillow, using ever curse word imaginable to describe how pissed I was. My suicide attempt was unsuccessful. I needed another way to release this pain.

In my mind and heart it felt like God was keeping me so this man could fuck me. I hated God so much for not letting me die. Everything I knew about God I didn't believe anymore because He left me with this cross to bare all alone and I was just a girl.

A kid.

While sitting in my room Indian style on my bed, I was thinking of other ways to take my life. It took an hour for an idea came to mind. I jumped up, went into my dad's bathroom to take a shaving razor. I didn't know how to release the blade at first since this was my first time trying to get the blade out of the container.

Dad used the double edge razor steel. My heart was beating so fast and every noise I heard I thought someone was coming inside my parent's room. As I pressed down harder on the release button for the blade to slide out, I was so nervous, I dropped it in the sink. The blade was so shiny, thin, and slippery. Once I picked it up with the tips of my fingers, I slowly put everything I touched back in the bathroom cabinet exactly the way I found it. I then went to the hallway bathroom. As I sat on the toilet, my hands were shaking and my eyes twitching back and forth. I was inhaling and exhaling, taking deep breaths in disbelief that this is really about to happen. *I'm really about to slit my wrist.* I closed my eyes and...

Cut.

Oh my goodness, I just cut my right thigh. Then, again I inhaled and exhaled before I turned my attention to my left leg.

Cut.

Blood started to seep out as I watched it drip down and around my thighs onto the floor. The pain…this pain gave me a rush. Felt like I was intoxicated, my mind had left my body and I had no worries. I sat back and took two more slashes out of my tights. This gave me the quick relief I was looking for. I felt like a mermaid swimming from sea to sea. The sharp sweetness of the cuts took away the haunting emotional trauma, at least for a few moments.

The cuts gave me a sort of inner peace. I sat there for few more minutes leaning back on the toilet. I rocked, arms crossed, and blood dripping. I immediate became concerned. How long could I keep this up before people began to notice when I put my shorts on to play basketball? I did not want to be in a position where I would have to explain why I had these scars. I had to find another way out fast.

7
Freshman Year

"Life without goals is like a race without a finish line."—Gareth McLean

The person I idolized most as a young teen was basketball star, Dawn Staley. I wanted to play just like her. I learned all her moves and I practiced from sun up to sun down. When it was time to choose a high school, I wanted to go to Murrell Dobbins Technical High School just like she did. I studied photography and accounting. For years, I was known to be able to look at numbers for a split second and memorize them without even trying so accounting was awesome for me. My passion for always hiding behind my eyes gave me the heart to grow to love photography. I've seen things in photos that other people didn't. Everyday at school, I stopped into the school gym to read the records Dawn had set, and envisioned my name on the walls next to hers.

Being a freshman wasn't easy for me, though. I hated school. I was one of those kids who never did homework or studied but passed tests. I had many friends because they thought I was funny and kind; however, I always thought they were laughing at me and not with me. They weren't really friends to me, not in high school. They were folks I entertained to make the time at school go by faster.

I wanted to play basketball for my high school team but, my grades were not good enough to play on the team that year, so I just watched the other girls train. I learn most of the plays and even some of the player's weak and strong sides of their game. I always told myself that I would be ready as a sophomore.

Once school was over for the day, I became someone different. I was dating Brian, smoking weed, and selling drugs for a local drug dealer name Paul. Paul was another friend of Derrick's who drove a 5-series, white, BMW. Paul always dressed like he was ready to a photo shoot. Derrick and his friends always thought I was the coolest so they never hid things from me. I saw all the dirty things they did from drugs to girls. People who saw me everyday had no idea what I was doing because I never did it in my neighborhood. In fact, I was never the type to flaunt money or buy popular clothing brands. Besides, sneakers were my drugs. Which wasn't any secret to my older siblings. I remember Derrick coming home from college one day saying, "Yo, sis, every time I see you, you always got some fly new basketball sneakers on and I know pops not buying those." I would simply laugh it off, tell him I did little odd jobs, and saved my cash. No one knew I hustled.

Derrick would have been upset if he knew that his friend let me hustle. There were times when it was late and someone needed something I would deliver the drugs on my bike to them. I even picked up a couple beers for my brothers and cousins when I was out. The Red Door was the spot to go to because they never carded you. That was when I learned it was all about who you knew.

The crazy thing was my siblings and I did any and everything we wanted to do once our mom went upstairs into her room. It was like clockwork. Everyday she would go in her room and never come downstairs until morning. We knew at a certain time we needed to take her something to eat or drink, and then we could disappear. When we did go back into the house, we would tiptoe and be as quiet as we could so she couldn't hear us. I never understood why she did that.

Being a part of something made me feel great. Dealing

drugs was my way of escaping home. Being around those drug dealers made me feel powerful but I was still hurting, just masking the pain behind the drugs and money. I never worried when I was in the street. They knew me as "Chevy" and no one bothered me. My reputation from middle, high school, and the neighborhood carried weight. I didn't want others to see me as this defenseless girl, so I began to carry a gun. At first, I didn't want to carry a gun since I had no experience with it and I didn't want any accidents. Once I picked it up it felt like a toy gun, and at that moment I knew what I wanted to do with it. This side of me gave me the control I needed but it allowed me to degrade and damage myself more. I started having sex. My first official partner was Brian. Brian and I started getting really close and we had grown to really like each other. Brian was different from my brothers. He helped me with my homework. He came to my basketball games and even came to my school to walk me home. He showed me he was into me. Those acts of kindness made me feel special and I didn't know how many ways to show appreciate for someone. So one night as Brian and I were talking, I confided in Brian about what Chester was doing to me. Brian was so upset that he paced back and forth talking to himself about ways to handle the situation. Brian started apologizing to me about how sorry he was that this was happening and that when he saw Chester he was going to beat his skull in. But first he wanted to tell my brothers and parents. Brian agreed to go with me to disclose this information to my parents. In fact, he was ready to expose Chester to everyone immediately and didn't hesitate. Brian grabbed my hand and proceeded to pull me towards his door. I begged and pleaded for him to let go and to not make me tell. I even told him about the threats that Chester had made but he didn't care. He wanted to protect me from it all. When Brian realized I wasn't budging he got upset with me. He didn't want to speak to me anymore. He threw up his hands and asked me to leave his house.

For a couple days we saw each other in passing and Brian didn't say one word to me. He didn't even look in my direction. It felt like eternality for me and I needed my friend back. Fast. He was the only real friend I had. So one late night, I called Brian's house phone and asked if I could come over to speak to him. As we sat on his bed, I began to cry about how hurt I was for him turning his back on me. He jumped up in a rage yelling at me about how he felt like I'm protecting Chester and I must be enjoying it that's why I haven't done or told anyone about it. With tears running down my face, I couldn't find all the words to say about how I wasn't protecting Chester and it was more so me protecting myself from everything and everyone that came with the exposure of the abuse. Brian didn't understand my position and didn't want to hear my explanation any longer. As he attempted to kick me out I beg for him not to and I lend in and kissed him. That night we had sex for the first time and we went on to maintain a secret relationship for three years and never talked about Chester again.

Besides, Chester was in for it. I had this gun and was hoping that when Chester's ass came home, I would be able to pull the trigger. But, where was he? It had been three weeks or so and I hadn't seen Chester around. I was starting to get used to him not coming around. The feeling of not looking over my shoulder or looking outside periodically to see if his van was out front was beginning to feel normal. It felt like I was becoming a normal teenager. Well, not completely normal, but nothing at this age could beat the feeling of not having to worry about his huge weight pressing in on me, to not think about his lousy breath whispering how special I was, or to be afraid to go to sleep because of the thoughts of his steps closing in. On this particular night, I slept so peaceful as if it all was a dream.

The next morning, I went off to school and the buses were on time. I participated in class. The teachers were impressed. My peers were nice and it felt normal to be normal. My world was finally rotating in my direction and my smile was authentic for the first time. I even got the OK that I was able to try out for the basketball team. Until a phone call that changed everything. I went to use the pay phone to call my mom to tell her that I would be late coming home due to basketball tryouts. But, her voice was different. She was speaking slowly as if she wanted me to hear every word clearly. With doubt in her voice she said, "You can't stay after school today and you need to make it home fast." My heart started to race and I couldn't catch my breath fast enough to ask her what had happened. Before I could get the words out she told me that Chester had enrolled into a rehabilitation center and he confided in a counselor. The next few words felt like a dream come true. She then said, "He told them that he was doing inappropriate things to someone close to him." My heart sank in disbelief as if it was finally over. Then, the moment of silence on the phone allowed me to hear her heavy breathing. The last statement I heard the tone of concern, not for me of course but for her foster children. I was not upset because that was how she made her living and it was being threatened by someone else's actions on her child. Then, all of a sudden she said, "The rehabilitation center immediately contacted Department Human Services (DHS) and a DHS worker was on their way to our house to interview you."

With no hesitation, I told her I was on my way. I jumped on the Number 33 bus, got off at 22nd Street and ran the rest of the way home thinking about what I was going to say. Part of me was at ease that it was finally over, but was it really over? I didn't know how to feel at this point. I started to feel bad and envisioned myself going to court, living in another home, and my parents losing everything because of me. My mother saved kids from the very abuse that I was subjected too. I did not want to hurt my family. I didn't want my mother to lose her foster children, so I felt I had to make a decision for the sake of the family.

My family.

I spoke to foster children and I knew the hell that some of them went through before being placed at my home. That scared me to death.

I opened the door and my mom was waiting with red eyes. "The lady is here," she said. The look she gave me told it all. My mind was made up to lie to this DHS worker. While the woman asked me questions I looked between her eyes and my mother's eyes before I responded. With every question, I lied with ease for the sake of the family. Was I wrong? I thought I was. How could I just do that? Did the worker believe him or me? I wondered what she thought about all this. I felt like shit after every question and thought about just bursting off the couch screaming and yelling, "Yes he hurt me. He did unspeakable thing to me like made me preform oral sex on him and threaten that if I hurt him he would hurt me worse. I didn't want to do it but he made me do it. What was I supposed to do? He also didn't want to get me pregnant so he would always pull out and cum somewhere on my body.

As my mother opened the front door to let the lady out she had a little grin on her face. The door closed behind her and on que my mother said, "I'm so happy you looked her in the eyes when you responded." With the look of relief on my mom's face, I turned, and walked away. From that day on, my mother never questioned as to why Chester would say such a thing.

8

It Got Worse Before It Got Better

It was the winter of 1998 and I was junior in high school. My parents moved my sister and I out of Philadelphia to New Jersey. This was the first time that I was out of the city. It was nice to finally be able to live in a beautiful place different than North Philadelphia. New Jersey was the new start that I needed. My cousins and I rode the New Jersey Transit to visit many of our family members who had moved here already. We had a back and front yard with grass, a driveway, and space. Neighbors didn't share our front steps and there was no metal fence or banister separating the neighbors front porch. I felt like we were finally able to live better and for my sister and I to not be looking over our shoulder while waiting at the bus stop or waiting to get robbed at the corner store.

It was a little struggle for me adapting and fitting in with all the other kids. First, I was in the eleventh grade coming into a new high school where many kids had built relationships with each other since elementary school. Then, I felt like I wore a I'm the new kid shirt everyday because people stared at me or kept asking where I was from. Or maybe I wore a magnet that only drew attention to the boys. One guy in particular was Eric.

Eric lived at the corner of my street. When we moved in he was playing basketball on a portable court with no backboard. Being from Philly I saw a lot of things but playing with no backboard was new to me. He was charming, cute, and short. He had a gold tooth and spoke with a Spanish accent. We played ball together on his no backboard court and my shot got better. I never looked at him in that way. This was really a start to a good friendship. My boy magnet made me have trouble with the girls since their boyfriends wanted to date me or liked me. I had a two boyfriends at this time, though. Brian and Stokley.

I had met Stokley the summer before I moved to New Jersey. He was a year older than me, about to graduate high school, and he wasn't in the street. Stokley's mother was cop so he was on the road to following his family's career path. He was quiet, reserved, and focused on his future. He had no

SCRAPES & SCARS

business liking me. Brian and Stokley knew each other since Stokley's cousin was Brian's neighbor. Brian didn't like Stokley and always called him a pretty boy. Stokley made it known that he like me to his cousin and was warned that I was Brian's girl. But Brian was in the street with different women and our relationship was a secret to my parents. So I decided to date Stokley. He was my first real boyfriend. The first boy, I was allowed to date based upon the rules of our home. Girls weren't allowed to date until they were sixteen.

Stokley and I didn't see or spend a lot of time together, but we did talk on the phone. When I moved my relationship with Stokley was forced to involve our parents because he was coming to visit me in another state and his mom had to pick him up a few times at the bus stop since the New Jersey transit ran differently from SEPTA on the weekends. His mother was nice enough to meet my parents and drop Stokley off for a couple hours on some Saturdays. We had fun when he did come and visit but Stokley was different. He had never had sex before and I was a confused little wild girl who only thought that guys showed how much they cared for you by having sex with you. Besides, I only dated Stokley to get back at Brian for running off and having a set of twins on me. One weekend I forced Stokley to have sex with me. I knew he didn't want to. and I had to show him how to do everything. Furthermore, the kind of attention that I needed

Stokley wasn't able to provide. So once we went on his prom together we immediately broke up and I never seen or heard from Stokley again.

Eric and I began to get close after Stokley's prom. I thought that Eric was jealous and I din't understand why when he had a girlfriend. She wanted to fight me when she found out that I was hung at the house playing ball with him. Nevertheless, one weekend Eric decided he wanted to let me know how he really felt after we hung out with some friends at Six Flags. Later that day, him and I had sex for the first time. Sex to me at the time was something to do. I didn't get anything out of it. For me, it was all about having control and feeding my desires.

One weekend in January, I visited Brian and stayed at my aunt Cece's house. Aunt Cece was cool she let me come and go as I pleased as long as I was back inside at a certain time. Sunday morning, while getting ready to go home, I stood at bottom of the steps looking in the mirror trying to put my hair in a ponytail. All of a sudden my shirt rose up and my aunt Cece was at the top of the stairs.

She saw my belly, raced down the stairs, and said, "Chick, are you pregnant?"

At first I had no idea. *Pregnant. Who me? Pregnant?* Hell, I really had no clue. All I knew was that when women got pregnant they no longer had a period. For the first six months, I did not feel a kick and I had a period. *Pregnant, I couldn't be.* Because my period was irregular, I knew it was late. It always came late. To this day, no one believed that I didn't know. I wore baggy clothes and I didn't see a rounded belly until aunt Cece pointed it out. Hell, I hardly looked at myself in mirror. I was not happy with who I saw so it was only for a moment when I did look in the mirror.

That Sunday was the longest day of my life, having to hear and see the disappointment on my parents face when they found out. My dad didn't want to speak to me and my mom felt ashamed—not that I was pregnant but ashamed at what people would say about me. Maybe not people but what her family thought about her teenage daughter being pregnant and still in high school. Not that my feeling mattered in any of this.

The next morning my mom and godmother took me to the doctors and that day changed me. I was so nervous going into the doctor's office. My heart beat fast and my nerves were all over the place. The doctor was nice and made me feel comfortable. All of the questions like when was your last period, are you sexually active, do you use protection made me feel uneasy because I didn't know. The doctor sensed the vibe that I was lost, so she started the exam. Yes, the urine came back positive for being pregnant. But my experience from the ultrasound had my heart jumping with joy. It was amazing when I first heard my daughter's heart beat. I felt and saw her kick me for the first time. It was full of emotion. In that moment, I was determined to give my baby the life that I had imagined for myself: a loving, compassionate, affectionate, reliable, and sincere mother.

From that day on, I refused to fail at anything. I couldn't fail because someone depended on me. But, then, reality hit and I failed. The first thing that I failed at was not knowing who was my daughter's father. Due to all the pain I lived with, I hurt myself by using men. I was very active and I used men for what they were good for. Now, I was faced with a problem. When my parents found out they were upset and disappointed but when the question of who the father was came up, this was where the real embarrassment came.

My parents were shocked because no one was expecting me to say, Brian's name. They wanted to kill him. My mom was upset and felt like he had taken advantage of me. He didn't. In fact, I took advantage of him now that I think about it. I pursued sex with him more than he did with me. Then, there was, Eric. My family didn't know anything about him and I having sex. All they knew was we went to the same school. We were neighbors and played basketball together. Nevertheless, I had to figure out a way to tell these two men what was going on.

SCRAPES & SCARS

I called Brian first to let him know and he was happy and overjoyed. Brian really liked me and felt a certain way that we had to sneak to be together. During our time together, he wanted to let my family know that we were dating, but I didn't want that to happen. Brian believed that my pregnancy was our chance to be together in the open. The following weekend my parents called a meeting with Brian's mother and it went well. With the exception of my parents feeling like Brian took advantage of me because he was older than me. Sadly, though, when he found out that he wasn't the only one he was confused and crushed. Even though, he was out there messing around the only boyfriend he knew about was Stokley. Now that Stokley wasn't in the picture Brian was devastated and we were ordered to stay away from each other.

When I broke the news to Eric he didn't care. He denied that we were even together. His parents never sat down with my parents. Eric wanted a DNA test before him and his parents claimed anything. Could you blame them? We pretty much avoided each other until the results came back.

9

Graduation Day

Finally, it arrived: graduation day. *Wow. I made it.* What a wonderful feeling to finally do something that could possible make your family proud, right? I had given birth to a healthy beautiful baby girl two months earlier and finished school, so that was an accomplishment. Considering the last couple months in my third trimester I was near death with sickness. I was homeschooled and my French teacher came out to my house to help me make my grade to graduate. I tortured her when I attended her class so I felt like she was paying me back by torturing me coming out to my house. Besides, all the other teachers just sent my work over for me to complete. Eric and my cousin took my work to school and turned it in for me.

Other than giving birth to my daughter, my graduation was the best day of my life. That afternoon while getting dressed, I was singing and having a great time with my daughter. She was too young to understand why I was happy. My oldest brother, William, and his girlfriend, Rasheeda, showed up and said they were attending graduation. I was in awe to see that they were coming to support me. Especially since, William was upset with me for getting pregnant. My dad was coming as well. This was going to be a night to remember I kept saying to myself as I put the final touches on my hair before heading out the door. We all laughed and talked in the car before they dropped me off at a separate entrance for the graduation.

Graduation was a big deal. Walking on the track and hearing all those people cheering on their loved ones was incredible. When my name was called to walk across the stage, hearing the chants go faint and feeling like everyone was talking about you as if they knew your secret devastated me. It was a horrible feeling. For the first time, I felt like I was on display and my evening was ruined. I had had a flashback on stage and I was no longer proud to be a graduate and I was left thinking about what had happened to me. Every time I looked at my daughter I was reminded of my innocence being stolen and no one knew it. No one cared. Or they knew it but never acknowledged it and tried to cover it up. The abuse from Chester had stopped but the wounds I carried weren't healing.

As graduation concluded and everyone was meeting up with their family I look everywhere but I couldn't find my family. Everyone was celebrating with their family and I was looking for mine. I learned that they had left early. I wasn't sure if they had seen me blackout walking across the stage. The look on my face when graduation was over and no one was there to hug me, bring me flowers, take a picture, say congratulations or anything hurt me to my bare bones. Too top it off I even had to bum a ride home. *Can you believe that shit?* I couldn't feel any lower than that. The feeling of not having someone around made my hate and dislike for my relatives grow stronger. I needed to get away before, I exploded. I didn't trust them at all anymore. That hurt. What hurts the most was not knowing why your own mother couldn't come to the graduation, but she never showed up for me. For a long time I expected her and I wanted her to be in my corner. I remember she went to all three of my brother's high school graduation and William's college graduation. The messed up part was Edward graduated two years after me and she went to his. What excuse can you give your child for that. It was disheartening. I didn't let them see me care but I suffered silently and I just took mental notes on how I was treated differently than everyone else. The feeling of not being good enough for my own mom affected me horribly. I went on and tried to live a normal life, so I enrolled into community college all alone with no support or help from relatives.

After high school graduation in the summer of 2000, while Brian and I were laying in bed together, after our parents told us not to, I received a phone call. It was Eric. His voice was so full of excitement and peace, and he didn't bother to say hello. He started the call with a demand: "I'm calling to let you that I just received the results of the DNA test and I need you to bring me my daughter."

My heart dropped.

I hung up the phone on Eric and called my mom. I asked if I received any mail. She said that the DNA test was there. She then started reading the results. When she read the results I froze and tears started to roll down my face. Brian sat up on the bed to ask me what was wrong but I couldn't find the right words. I began to stutter, and then, it hit me to be upfront. I'm mentally prepared to tell Brian about the results of the test to his face. Why? Life isn't being fair to me. Brian loved my daughter and he treated her like his own since I had her. He spent more time with her than Eric had. Brian and I never talked about the possibility of her not being his maybe we should have so I would have been prepared for this moment.

As I hung up the phone and looked Brian in his eyes I said, "Brian I am so sorry, but she isn't your daughter."

The look on his face was filled with disbelief, defeat, and hurt. Brian said nothing. He slowly got off the bed, packed our things, and told me he never wanted to see me again. I was broken because I genuinely liked him, but it was so hard explaining how I was sleeping around and why I made those choices. During that time, I didn't really know what was going on with me. He told me he forgave me but he wanted nothing to do with me ever again. I couldn't be mad at him. I just didn't want to let go because I was afraid of what he could do with my secret. Nevertheless, that was the consequence for my behavior. I deserved it. I deserved all of the rage, pain, and hurt I was going through.

This time I was the abuser; hurting and abusing others emotionally. This was my second introduction into adulthood and it marked the last time I blamed my past for my present behavior. I realized I could not play the victim card any longer. Adulthood meant being responsible for one's actions. I could not afford to be so reckless anymore. I didn't want to blame anyone because the pain I caused people was what I had to bear. It was rough learning to live with the guilt of being an abuser of myself and to others. I knew it was going to be a long road but I was ready for it. I had to push the little girl inside off to go sit in the corner and I needed to allow my scrapes and scars to heal properly. I had no clue how to find a way to rise above my tears, to rise above my hurt, abuse and violations of myself; it was the beginning of a new world for me, I thought I could do it on my own. Then Brian kissed my daughter for the last time and we parted ways.

Few weeks after breaking the news to Brian, I moved out of my parents' house with my daughter and Eric and I got an apartment together. My relationship with my parents —or should I say mother—was spiraling out of control and I was just wasting time continuing to hurt myself by staying there. Searching for her approval and love was beginning to become exhausting. No one understood me so it caused a lot of confusion and fights.

During that time moving in with Eric felt like the right thing to do. I was under the impression that we were going to ride off into the sunset together. Eric was the sweetest guy at first, but then life happened, and we started living and having to be responsible for people and things changed. We started having arguments out of nowhere; at least at the time that's what I thought. I left one abusive home for another one. The mental, physical and emotional abuse that we both put on each other was real and I had no one to share my pain with. Or maybe I was too embarrassed to say anything because I was afraid how people would look at me a certain way. I never wanted people to feel sorry for me. Not as a kid and surely not as an adult. So, on the outside it looked like I had a loving boyfriend who spoiled me with cars, money, and jewelry, but on the inside I was suffering. At night, I hardly slept and during the day, I kept myself busy so I wouldn't think about everything that was bothering me. I learned early on how to adapt to any environment that I was in and not to show any fear or emotions.

Trying to live a normal life while broken was hard. I couldn't stop my past from haunting me. So I turned to more alcohol and continued smoking. Eric had no idea what I was doing to myself. I hid this life from everyone. Once the alcohol and my high wore off, the thoughts still showed up to torture me. Suicidal thoughts began to cloud my mind ever moment of the day. This was the first time since I had my daughter that death seemed like my only way out. Then, I began to get angry with the drugs and alcohol not realizing that it was a mixed emotion drug and people became more depressed once their high was over.

Months turned into years and I wanted out of the relationship but I didn't know how to leave. Everyday it was a new fight and new argument. In my head, I had all the words but my mouth couldn't say them. I knew I couldn't go back home because I didn't like it there. I believed my dad didn't care if I was home, but it was her, my mother, who never wanted me in the first place. She never said those words but she treated me like that. When I did visit to get away for a few days, she made it very uncomfortable so I continued to play house with Eric while suffering from depression in silence.

My past had showed up and showed out more often since being with Eric. While being in our apartment alone and when my daughter was taking her naps, I felt like the walls were closing in on me. It was hard to concentrate on anything but the thoughts of Chester. The smell of his sweat and cigarettes flooded my house and the overwhelming feeling of hopelessness invaded my headspace. No amount of bleach, incenses or candles dissolved his scent. It was forever embedded in my nostrils. I was afraid to leave my daughter with a babysitter, my parents or anyone, because I felt like everyone was a suspect and had the ability to hurt my child. And I couldn't live with that pain of anyone hurting my baby the way he hurt me.

When I started working at a daycare, my daughter went to work with me some days. On others she stayed with my mom—against my better judgment, but what was a girl to do —and the other children she cared for. I had to make sure I had some sort of control in the environment she stayed in, albeit there was no control that protected me in that same household. On my lunch breaks, I went to my parent's house to check on her.

CHAVONNE HURDLE

* * *

As if all that wasn't enough, I was struggling with another issue. I had an addiction to sex. I needed and desired it ever hour and second of the day. The more I talked myself out of it the more I saw it in everything. Eric didn't know I was struggling. He tried his best to fulfill my needs but it wouldn't go away. Eric was beginning to get frustrated with me and I was beyond frustrated with him so I had to find someway to fulfill these needs, and it had to be fast.

Daniel was his name.

Daniel was a friend who I met the summer of 2000. He was twelve years older than me and married with four kids. Daniel was fine. He had glassy eyes, white teeth, silky black hair, and a walk with him that would put Barack Obama's walk to shame. He was so charismatic and that made him all the more attractive. I had a crush on his nephew, but his nephew had a girlfriend. Daniel didn't seem to mind talking to me every chance we saw each other. It didn't matter, he was checking for me and I knew it.

One day leaving work early, I was driving and saw Daniel. He invited me come over to his house while his wife was at work. During my visit, we had small talk about life plans and goals. I didn't let him know that I was broken. We laughed at how he thought his nephew was scared of girls, how he was too young, and shouldn't settle down. Daniel and I talked for about thirty minutes about absolutely nothing. As I was getting ready to leave, I walked towards the door and Daniel said, "You should be my girlfriend and I would take care of you. All you have to do is be available for me whenever I need you to be."

In my head, I'm thinking this sounds like something I've seen from a movie. The proposal was also what I needed in my life to fulfill my own desires. I had never been propositioned like this before and I needed to think about what he was being asked of me. I had never dated a married man before either and I was confused by the amount of karma that would come my way if I did this.

I played it cool and told him that I needed some time to think about this and as I reached for the door he grabbed my hand. He threw me up against the wall, started kissing me with so much passion, that I couldn't resist or fight him off. I didn't know how to tell him to stop and didn't want to fight him off. My mind was racing fast and my body was melting. I wanted him to stop but I couldn't find the words or the voice to say it.

This was the start of something I wanted no parts of but had no idea how to get out of it. This relationship went on for eight years. Before I would see him I would take a couple shots of vodka and a few pulls of weed. Once our session was over I would go home, sit in the tub and soak for hours, drinking and wondering: *why the hell am I doing this to myself again.*

Daniel took care of me too. He made sure I had hundreds of dollars in my account, he brought me a car, and made sure my daughter had everything she needed. It seemed like every other day I would call and break it off with Daniel and he would call me a few days later and tell me a time to meet him and I would be there. There was a time that I was driving home and I asked myself was why was I so afraid to say, "No."

Then I thought back to my childhood.

The behavior that I was exhibiting was bothersome to me and Eric. He had no idea what I was doing at night or while he was at work, but he had an idea that something wasn't right with me and he didn't know how to ask. Therefore, we just fought all the time. We both had no clear vision as to what to do or where to go. He was the only one who loved me so I felt like this is somewhere I needed to be. I couldn't leave him, because he needed me like I needed him. In the mist of abusing myself, I couldn't tell people I knew but I found peace talking to strangers.

For a year and a half, I would call a domestic abuse

SCRAPES & SCARS

hotline and speak with counselors about options on how I could deal with the frequent memories of Chester and how I could leave Eric. I especially wanted to leave Eric after he made me abort our twins and after getting me pregnant again, giving birth to our second daughter. I also sought advice on how to break the cycle of abuse from Daniel.

I remember the last call I made to the hotline a much older lady answered the phone. She was well spoken, had a great deal of knowledge, and was very resourceful. However, she also gave me devastating news. During our conversation about Chester she told me that there was a thing called statute of limitation on child molestation and rape cases. Why didn't anyone tell me this sooner? Have I been asking the wrong questions all this time? I was in shock, disbelief and speechless. In my naïve mind I figured things like this could last a lifetime and whenever a person wanted to come forward they could. Justice was going to prevail no matter the time that passed. But no it didn't work like that, I had learned. That was another gut wrenching shot and I wanted to die. I couldn't believe that he was getting away with all of the pain that he has caused me.

When I felt ready to be honest with someone and open up about what happen, hear she was telling me I couldn't get him arrested. I felt my life sinking deeper and deeper and I couldn't breathe. It's too late. *It's too late.* Why me God? She sat on the phone and listened to my cries and how broken down I was. Then I begun to scream, "Oh my goodness, this is my fault and I should have told when I had the chance as a teenager when someone would have believed me." *How am I supposed to go on living now?* The lady on the phone said, "Everyone will believe you here just come into the shelter to get help we can help you young lady. Trust us."

In my mind everything was messed up. I hung up and begin to drown myself in alcohol. My daughters were in the other room crying because they heard me yelling. I slowly walked calmly into their room, after I dried my face with my shirt. My oldest daughter always had a way of knowing when I was hurting and she would always cry when I cried. I opened their room door and their they were two incident girls looking at me, expecting me to take care of them. All I could do was hug and love on them smelling like a drunk. They didn't care how I smelled they loved their mommy.

After finding out the bad news later that night, Eric and I had a huge fight, and I needed to leave. I was ready to leave there but had no place to go. My kids were crying and if I had a gun I would have blown my head off. *What am I going do now?* Without thinking I picked up the phone and called the local police station and told them I needed an escort to the shelter. Without question they told me come to the precinct. Eric had left for work so it was the perfect time to disappear forever. Once I got there, they escorted my children and I to the shelter.

With my mind racing a mile a minute and everything moving fast around me, here I am answering question about my past and present to this stranger in this strange place. With great embarrassment, I knew I had to keep this secret because every other time I would leave Eric and when I visit my parents she would allow Eric to stay at her house and sleep on the couch until I was ready to come home. I didn't want him coming around anymore; and I just wanted to be free of him. So I didn't tell my parents where I was but I did tell my college counselor she even called and checked on me.

In the shelter, I experienced how strong I really was for my children and myself. My two daughters needed to see something positive from me. For most of their life they had seen and heard negativity. There had to be something different I could show them. But I needed to take care of me first so I could show them. There were all types of women living in the shelter. I couldn't imagine living there again. That experience changed my life forever.

After being in the shelter for a day without talking to anyone it was important to get acquainted and become familiar with the house and the rules. My first group meeting and introduction to the house this woman came into the community room with so much joy, charisma. She demanded everyone's attention with her sweet voice. This was my first merry-go-round with group counseling. It was amazing and I was amazed how this woman controlled the room and the conversation. I had no idea about this world but I knew I wanted to learn more and be a part of it.

During group I stood out like a short person in a room full of tall people. I didn't participate. I just sat and listened. Soaking up all the information I could. Once the meeting was over, the counselor called me into her office. That was the moment of truth. I sat there for thirty minutes, which felt like three hours, and I told her why I was there, why I needed to leave my old life, and how my future was going to be. Whatever I said captivated her and she wanted to know the little girl behind the young lady. She didn't want my mask on. She wanted to know Chavonne and demanded that. We spent a lot of time together just talking. She was so nice and she didn't make me feel like the trauma in my life was my fault. I told her about my dreams of being successful, going back to college, buying my own home, working in a prison as a correctional officer, and buying my own car. Yes, I had had cars but I always had men buy me cars and a home. If I had my own, I certainly wouldn't be living here. I wanted to work hard so my children could have a positive, successful, honorable woman to look up to. This was why I loved her so much. She was one of the positive, educated, humble, women who came into my life, who showed me how to conduct myself as a woman who wanted something out of life.

She told me that once I got out of the shelter, I needed to speak to someone about what I been through, talk to God, and start living. Indeed I did.

Within thirty days of leaving the shelter, I moved into my own apartment. How I received the apartment was beyond me. A woman who was providing food to the shelter had an apartment complex. I believe she had seen something in me that made her want to help me. We never had a conversation, though. Indeed, I am forever grateful to her for blessing me. I also found a counselor and began my journey to becoming a better me. It was so hard. I was alone and couldn't really tell anyone what I was going through because of the stigma that counseling and getting help held in the African-American community.

This was the first time in my life, I was living on my own, and finally was able to look at myself in the mirror and be proud of me. Proud of who I was becoming for my daughters. I struggled for a few months and was still learning how to budget my money, balance a checkbook, to not buy things I didn't need. I learned these skills living at the shelter. At the time, I was still working at the day care and part-time as radio dispatcher at the local community college. I managed to make sure all of my bills were paid on time, food in the refrigerator, a couple dollars in my account, and gas in my car to make it back and forth to work each day.

After a while, seeing my counselor started to become more of job and I felt like I needed a break. Plus, I danced around a lot of important issues like trying to work on a relationship with my mother and father since I knew that the would never go for coming to counseling.

Eric and I had been a part for six months and he had enlisted in the army to keep from getting in trouble. We spoke on the phone here and there and he seemed like he was a changed person. I talked as if I was stronger than ever and all our problems were gone. There I was putting my mask back on and not showing him who I truly was. I thought we were on the right track, so we got back together.

Soon after getting back together we decided to get married after Eric finished boot camp. Two weeks after, we move to Tennessee while Eric was stationed in Kentucky. My last session with my counselor I told her about my addiction since I was moving and would never see her again, she recommend that I see a sex therapist. I couldn't believe it. I began to talk myself out of the truth. Denial was never good. The way she used addiction and the way I used it was different. Her words did resonate with me at first because sex was something everyone did and liked, right? I liked sex also but addicted I couldn't see it. Yes, I desired it every moment of the day but didn't everyone? Well, maybe not all the time because I was never satisfied. Better yet, didn't people who had anxiety and stress resort to sex to make them selves feel better? I used sex as a way to get my mind off the hurt and pain that I felt when those thoughts of abuse came to mind. Just like I would when I drank and smoked. I needed an immediate sense of control and someone to validate me and provide relief from those thoughts. Sex did all of those things for me. It was a high that I never wanted to come down from.

In the meantime, while struggling with my addiction to sex, I helped Eric be the best army man he could be. I helped him with school so he could get promotions and be great at his job. He promised that once he finished his career I would be able to start mine. The kids were too young and I wasn't OK with them going into day care in this strange place so I stayed home with the girls. Besides, Eric didn't want me to work. While at home, I began to feel worthless. I needed something that was mine. Something I put my heart, blood, sweat, and tears into. I smiled and made life look great on the outside but I was hurting. Still hurting. I was an addict and desired it all day and night. Soon I started out on the Internet and learned ways to curve my addictions and appetite. Self-pleasures. It was better than abusing someone else.

Eight months later, Eric left to do his first tour in Iraq.

CHAVONNE HURDLE

In the summer of 2005, I came home from Clarksville, Tennessee to have a good time and see my relatives and friends. Tennessee was far away from my friends and I needed to have some time without the kids. So I called my girls and told them we are hitting the streets of Philadelphia. All my friends were excited to see me and I was happy to see familiar faces. Then, all of a sudden, I saw this guy walking towards me. I couldn't see his face clearly, but I knew the walk. It was Brian. I hadn't seen or heard from him in five years and all those nights I practiced what I would say if I ever saw him again. Now I was at a loss for words.

Staring at me, he said, "I need to talk to you right now."

I was so nervous and everyone who was standing around and someone loudly said, "Ooohhh, what did she do?"

My girlfriend I was with said, "Girl, you need to go see what he talking about."

We walked down the street and sat on an abandoned house steps. Before I could ask him what this was about he quickly said, "Where the hell is my daughter?"

I gave him a strange look. I had to think back to when I told him I had gotten the results five years ago.

He gave a quick stare and continued, "I know you let some nigga adopt my daughter." He pulled out his wallet and started showing me the pictures that he had of my daughter from when she was a baby that I had mailed to him years ago. I asked him who had told him that someone adopted my daughter. He told me he had called my parent's house a few years ago and my mother told him I didn't live there anymore, and he had thought she was lying so he had my uncle John call while he was on a three-way.

When my mother answered the phone she immediately started having small talk with my uncle John and then he asked where I was. She started to talk about how I had moved to Tennessee and had a beautiful wedding before I relocated and allowed Eric to adopt Brian's daughter.

I sat there in shock as he told me the story. He was angry and he wanted answers. He sat there on the step with hurt in his eyes and for the life of me I couldn't understand why. "I'm not lying, Chavonne he said to me. "Your mom hated me since she found out we were sleeping together and she would have done anything to make sure I had no parts of your daughter life."

At first, I told him to stop lying but he suggested I call my mother and his mother to confirm. I couldn't imagine why he would lie so I took him up on his offer to call his mom and she confirmed. She was happy to hear from me and wanted to know where her grand baby was. With so many thoughts, all I wanted to do was leave. I couldn't produce the paternity test after five years. The paper was long gone. All these years had passed and he thought my mother lied about the paternity test when she told me the results over the phone since he had never physically seen the paperwork for himself. But I couldn't understand why he thought that Eric conspired with my mom. That didn't make sense to me. I sat there sad and embarrassed that I had to defend someone's actions. I couldn't understand why my mother would tell him such a lie. At first I wasn't really sure that she would even say something like that, but then I thought back to the night when he and his mother sat in our living room talking about me getting pregnant and the real issue with my mother had been his age. I realized there was the possibility of her telling him that story.

Five years later, I was being forced to go through this all over again. As I was about to leave he asked if he could see a picture of what my daughter looked like. I showed a picture to him, and it only reassured him that she was his and I did not want him to be a part of her life.

But what could I do now? After all he never wanted to see me again. I don't owe him anything. *Or did I?* I had moved on with my life and I did not have anything to prove. I truly felt bad but I wasn't going to put my daughter or Eric through that again. But, I needed to give him and his mother closure I owed them that. *Or did I?*

SCRAPES & SCARS

How was I going to tell Eric that I ran into my old boyfriend who I cheated on him with five years ago, that he wanted a paternity test while he was over in Iraq fighting for our country? *I'm not doing that...*

10

When It Became Real for HER

"Mother's love is peace. It need not be acquired, it need not be deserved."—Erich Fromm

I was twenty-eight-years-old, married, and now had three kids living in Texas. Eric deployed again so I decided to go visit my parents in New Jersey for awhile. One afternoon, I got a phone call at work from was my mother. She wanted me to come over; she had something to talk to me about.

I drove over there wondering what in hell's name she could possibly want from me. It was less than rare to have her call me, so of course, it was pretty typical of me to wonder what she could want. I had not did or said anything to anyone lately so what could this talk be about and the urgency for it?

I could not call Eric because he was deployed to Iraq so I was all alone and there was no one at all to help prep me for the bullshit.

Bullshit: Talk nonsense to someone, typically to be misleading or deceptive.

As I parked my car, I prayed: *Do not let me be quick to speak or anger, Lord fill me with a humbling spirit.* I walked down the hall in utter nervousness. I went into their bedroom and she was there lying on the bed with my dad sitting on the edge.

Immediately, Dad said, "Close the door."

"Did he really do it?" My mom asked instantly.

In a quick response, I said, "Did what and who are you talking about?"

"Chester, did he..." She cleared her throat before continuing. "Did he really molest you?"

I took a deep breath to collect my thoughts. "Yes, he did," I said.

"When and where? Tell me about the days and times

when this happened." She responded harshly.

At first I wanted to say all these years have passed and you are concerned now? Now that I am a married woman, you want to set your soul free or something? I don't need you or my father's protection anymore. Most importantly, I don't need a mother—those days are long gone. But, I gave her what she wanted, all the moments that had been stolen from my life. I made sure that the incidents that I gave couldn't be questioned because he almost got caught and when my dad walked in when the fire broke out was the icing on the cake, I thought. But to my surprise the incident with the social worker I stated and all this time my dad never knew it happened. I stood there and watched the bullshit on both their faces. I held both of them equally responsible. In my head, all I thought was *now you know so what you going to do?* Well, the answer to this was NOTHING.

When Chester wanted to come over to the house she would tell me he was coming and I could either leave or go into another room. What type of mother would ignore her child again? What type? I failed to understand (now that I am a mother myself) how could she possibly sleep at night? All I ever wanted for my life was for my mother to embrace me, lay in my bed with me, and cry about how sorry she was that this had happened to me. I wanted to hear her hurt and try to feel her pain for me being violated. I wanted to hear how she was going to kill that motherfucker the next time she saw him. I wanted to hear the hurt and pain from my mother, but it never came. She never even cried. She never did lie down with me. She never did express her hatred for Chester. Perhaps that was why I never felt her love for me.

She remained faithful to Chester. Sadly, she made a fateful choice. She made her decision and that was choosing him over me—her own daughter. The moment she consciously made her decision, she lost her oldest daughter forever. That was the first time I realized she did not give two shits about me. It sucked because no matter where I lived in the world, I always came home. Not for me, but for my children, or maybe it was for me. I needed her but I hated who she had been for me but I continued to give her chances to be my mother again, with slight hopes that maybe one day, she would be a mother to me in the real sense of that word. I never wanted my children to be devoid of a relationship with their grandparents either. But mostly, I wanted her to see that I was a better mother than she ever was to me. Revenge.

And on top of the not giving two shits about me, I was leaving town and needed a ride to the airport as my ride cancelled last minute. I told my mom about my struggle to find a ride, not that I wanted her to find someone, but just for mere conversation. I didn't want to pay the last minute shuttle fees but I was. Nevertheless, moments later, she called me to her room to tell me that she had found me a ride. filled with excitement.

I asked who it was.

She said, "Chester offered to take you."

I just stared at her and thought, *"Bitch, are you out your damn mind to even ask Chester?"* I wanted to scream that at her. But I did not. I simply stood there and looked at her in abject disbelief and sadness for her. I was at an age where I could see clearly her struggle between right and wrong. I knew that she did what she did because that's all she knew how to do. This was it, I accepted her for who she was, and met her at the place she was in. But the child inside of me wanted to ask her so many questions. How could you fix your lips to ask him? Did you ever care that he not only molested me but raped me and stole my ability to make sound judgments as it related to sex and relationships? Just what kind of cold, conniving mother would do this to her daughter? Was she trying to deliberately patch-up the relationship between her and her abuser?

11

Stranded

Stranded: "Left without the means to move."

Kicking and screaming my way through eight years of marriage was hard. By the time I turned thirty-years-old, I wasn't sure how I managed to stay married this long. I could no longer pretend or hide who I was from anyone. I found myself giving less and less each day to everyone.

One day at nine in the morning, after the kids were off to school, I sat on the back porch, enjoying the stiff Virginia breeze, and my favorite hard liquor. *This has to stop*, I thought, even though, I continued to sip wine and take shots of hard liquor. I could not continue to drink alcohol like it was coffee in the morning. More important, I could not show up to my counseling session reeking of booze again.

They will take my children away from me and I will be dammed to hell and back before they give them to my mom, I thought. *She could never raise my children. Hell, she did not even raise me.* Over my dead body would she be in the driver's seat of my children's lives. Figuring out ways to change my life before I lose my children was hard. Listening to people tell me what to do was even harder. I felt like I had to figure it out on my own since people felt entitled to brag when they offered help and I accepted.

All I ever wanted was to change my life, my body, and my family. The most recurring question, though, was: *Where would I start?* Eric did three tours of war and it seemed like every year when he came back from the war I was forced to learn someone new. I began to drink more and more. I went from starting to drink at 6 p.m. to starting at 9 a.m. It was bad and I knew I was headed down the wrong road.

He changed and he had an excuse for it. He blamed the war and never wanted to get help. He distanced himself from the children and I for some time. I had to deal with those changes, all bad or indifferent. But it only brought out more thoughts of what I had went through. I needed help again. I was changing too and was not totally healed because I did the work sporadically and not consistently. Our love life had crashed and my desires were growing stronger and stronger and I was about to explode. But my kids needed me because I was their only parent while he went off to save the world and grieve his friends he lost during the war right before coming back home. I didn't understand him and he didn't understand me. We barely talked to each other and it was beginning to show around the children. I needed to do something fast.

I confronted Eric and told him I needed to go get a job and he stated, "He provides everything I need and me going to get a job is messing up the plan he set up years ago."

I couldn't take it any longer so I went out against his plan and searched for any job, as long it wasn't inside our home waiting on Eric all day and night like I'm his damn maid. Few days later, I took an evening shift at JCPenny and enrolled in college online.

One night when I got home from work, Eric was waiting up for me. I knew this wasn't be good. One argument lead to another and we had a fight.

I called the police.

I knew that this was it.

Our relationship was over and there was no turning back. Eric left before the police arrived and I walked the halls all night trying to come up with a plan for my life. The next day, I went to the military base tipsy to speak with my counselor and family advocate about helping me cope with my husband, my childhood trauma, and my addiction to sex. I was ready to put it all on the table. Everything was gone. I had nothing to lose. No family. I isolated myself from friends because they didn't understand why I stayed with Eric so long. The counselor told me, first, I needed to figure out if I was going to remain in my marriage. If not, then, I needed to come up with a safety plan to exit. Then, I had to figure out where I was going to live because I didn't have a decent job and all our money was Eric's. I hid money for a rainy day but it wasn't enough to put a down payment on a place and live for a few months until a job came through. During that session, I wrote out a plan for my life.

The next day, I saw the psychiatrist who wrote out my diagnoses as Generalized Anxiety Disorder and depression. We talked about the addiction but I told her I wanted to see if I could do this on my own before I see anyone. Something inside of me was more dedicated to doing the work now then ever before. I was still too embarrassed to talk about the addiction to sex. On the drive home all I could think was how I wished this was a bad dream and how was I going to make some money to move out. When I got home I immediately put my furniture up for sale on Craigslist. I didn't expect to sell it the same day but it did and I started putting things in motion. That night, I laid in the bed and pulled out the plans, I had written, and read aloud to the psychiatrist.

The first course of action was to leave Eric. Secondly, tell my kids that we would be OK, I loved them, and they needed to trust me. Thirdly, find a job. Fourth, finish school. Fifth, buy a house for my babies. Six, buy myself a car. Seventh, get help with my addiction. Eight, build a relationship with God. Last but not least take a minute to breathe because I had to set another to-do list. The next day, I bought some tote boxes and met with Eric to tell him that in the morning I was moving out. We cried together but knew that it was for the best.

12

Rock Bottom

Disoriented: "To confuse by removing or obscuring something that has guided a person, group, or culture, as customs, and moral standard."

Around 5:30 in the morning me and my three kids were packed in the truck and ready for another episode of what this cold world had to offer. The night before, I contacted my father and told him what was going on and he told me that I could come back home.

Moving back home with my parents in New Jersey after leaving, I couldn't take it but looking at my children I had no choice. This was another setback and I had to start from ground zero. I had definitely hit rock bottom. But, my pride was put to the side because I was broken into many little pieces. I was a mother who couldn't live another day in agony. I had made a good choice. A good one. During that six-hour drive, I cried, and started looking for God.

Home for me was never a good idea. It lacked space and love. For that time, I had to sleep in a bottom bunk with my kids for the first few days, then, I got a mattress from a friend slept on the living room floor out in the open. In that moment, I understood the adage *beggars can't be choosy*. That forced me into a deeper depression. I felt worthless and guilty that I did this to my children. For days, I couldn't eat anything. I was always agitated, sad, and thoughts of suicide clouded my mind again. I went on several job interviews but nothing was coming through for me. I kept my goal list in my pocketbook and looked at it multiply times a day so I wouldn't lose focus.

Eric and I were legally separated and he made every attempt to make me feel the pain of the separation. But I refused to go back to him this time, so we fought it out in court, which felt like an eternity. I was determined to show him that I didn't need him for anything anymore. The high school girl he had first met was gone and the woman in me was here to stay. Since I was a stay at home mom he was forced to pay child support and spousal support. He didn't like that at all and he tired everything in his power to take that away.

A few weeks later, my sister had given her job a good reference about me, and they hired me. Her job was an hour and fifteen minutes away from my parents' house and I worked evenings for a home security dispatch company. One night I came home late and my son was fighting to stay awake just so he could see me. He told me that he didn't see me anymore. My heart was broken. My children were used to me being there for them, picking them up from school, helping with homework, us spending time together, and now they had no idea who I was or where I was.

That night I cried. I couldn't stop crying. This was the first time since being back home that I allowed myself to feel the pain I was hiding. I finally broke down. I realized my reality was staring me in the face with beautiful eyes. I needed to accept who I was, where I've been, what I've done to focused on who I was becoming and where I'm going. I received my second wind and was ready for the world.

That next morning, I called my old supervisor at the community college and told them my situation. They were happy to hear from me and without hesitation they re-hired me within two weeks. That was the jump-start I needed. I quit the other job since it was to far to travel. The more good things happened to me, more worse things happened. I couldn't catch a break. My truck had broken down on my way leaving the last night of my quitting the job. The repairs cost $3000. And to top that, my daughter's necklace was stolen.

My children and I were already living out of tote boxes at my parent's house. We didn't have our own space. The necklace was missing for a few days before anyone told me about it. The feeling of failing as a parent was a hard pill to swallow. And I was trying my best to swallow it. I put my kids in a situation for things to be taking from them as if they haven't lost enough. I couldn't bare to see them lose out on anything else.

That day I packed our things and I move out of my parents' house. I had no idea where I was going. I just knew I couldn't stay there any longer. I got my kids and we headed to bible study as if nothing happened. My kids went into the church and I sat in the car and just broke down again asking God, "What have I done so bad in my life to deserve all that I'm receiving from it." I refused to go inside of the church. About thirty-five minutes later, a friend in the church came out and she walked me inside. I just sat there soaking in my pain blocking out God's word and trying to figure out where the hell I was going to sleep.

I didn't want to do it but I had no choice, so once bible study was over I called my best friend and asked if I could stay at her place for a few weeks. She obliged and I slept on her couch while my babies slept in her son's room on the floor. This was another hurdle I was forced to get over. The shame and the stress of being homeless made me lose thirty-five pounds and I was forced to go to the hospital. Leaving the hospital all I wanted to do was drive my car off the bridge. I had had enough. Every corner I turned I hit a wall and bust my head wide open. I couldn't take it anymore. I couldn't catch a break. I was ready to go.

One day, I called my friend (counselor) whom I met my first year in community college and I told her the news as I walked around the neighborhood until things begin to look unfamiliar. Everything had taking a toll on me. She told me, "Hey, listen, it's OK and it will be OK. You will be fine. You will get through this like everything else." I never told her about my thoughts of dying that night and how her words played over and over in my mind. That was the last night I ever thought about suicide again.

That Sunday my children and I met my godmother for church service. Every song by the praise and worship team felt like they was for me. My bones shook. I rocked in my chair and cried. I sat in the chair with my head in my hands on my lap crying and praying the entire service. I remember my God mom coming over to me saying, "Everything you've been carrying is being lifted off your back right now.

Just telling that story always makes me cry because that

was the start of something real for the first time in my life. I felt protected, painless, and in that moment, I felt everything being lifted off my shoulders, back, and neck that had weighed me down for decades as I walked to the altar to give my life to Christ.

That day, I felt that things were going to be OK. I knew that all the suffering was over, I would live for me, and be a wonderful mother to my children. My children watched me do my best when I thought it was never good enough. Soon after that experience, I found us a house. My divorce became final after three years of pure hell, and I was offered a job in Virginia as a Correctional Officer. That same year as I was rebuilding my life, I met this fine man of God, who never once looked at me as less of a woman but a strong woman who was destined to be great. A year later, I graduated from Liberty University with my B.S. in Criminal Justice. And a year after that I graduated with my M.A in Marriage and Family Counseling. Life was finally on track.

13

REWIND

A person having their innocence taken away at a young age gives them a depth of perspective, albeit in a negative way. It also changes them in areas one could never imagine. For me, it wasn't until I became mature enough to understand how this tragedy had affected me. My rape and parents neglect affected my ability to comfort, love, respect, and trust my own self at times. All my life, I wondered how my parents would explain to me how sorry they were for not paying attention to the signs that something was happening to me. I was their daughter, meaning they were responsible for caring and protecting me. But they didn't.

There was no excuse my parents could give for their

neglect. Their negligence cost me not only my childhood but also the early years of my adult life. This was not something that went away.

EVER.

My parents saw me everyday and failed to notice anything different? I was left with many questions starting with:

How could my parents never notice the signs?

Why did Chester choose to steal my innocence?

How many other children had he violated?

Why didn't my mother question closer after the DHS worker left our house, after this man claimed to have raped someone in the house. One of the kids were a victim, so why didn't she try to figure it out.

These questions like all other unanswered questions entangled with my dreaded childhood memories continued to haunt me. For years, I couldn't look at myself in the mirror since I disliked my mother so much. I felt like I looked so much like her so hating her meant hating myself.

For most of my life, I walked around feeling like I was different and an outcast from my family because I was molested and raped. I felt like I didn't have any family. I lost trust and hope in everyone who shared Chester's last name. I felt like they smiled in my face and talked behind my back.

When they found out no one came to me and said sorry or anything. I had nothing left for myself either. I didn't care though because everyone owed me. So my attitude and how I treated people was their own fault. I was going to take what was owed to me one way or another. There were a chosen few of people whom I knew God placed in my life to help me. Those people I kept at a distance and if anything had happened to me they all would have known.

The worst part about the pain was that in most cases victims were left to deal with this alone. Just as I was and I became untrusting, believing no one could keep me safe. But, I did my best to be brave, put on a smile and pretend like everything was OK. That didn't get me far.

14
Lasting Effects

I don't think anyone that's not educated on the subject or have personal experience understands the magnitude of pain and trauma that being sexually abused, molested and raped has on a person. This pain will never hurt like the initial contact of breaking the skin, but the scar of a broken and shattered flesh will always remain. It does something to your mind and at times when you think you have control you really do not.

I suffered from panic attacks and often re-victimized myself by not having the ability to say "NO" at times. The fear of being awaken from my sleep by someone prying into my privates caused me to stay up majority of the night; when I did fall asleep the softest noise would wake me up and I could not go back to sleep. To get a good uninterrupted sleep I would have to take my prescribed sleeping pills.

My inability to trust people, family included is hard. I'm learning more and more everyday, as I grow even older. I struggle with my children being around my male friends, my father, my brothers, my husband or even them hanging out with their friends because of my fear of them being sexual abused, raped and molested like me.

For decades, I had strong issues with intimacy and self-loathing. I had a fear of being touched too strongly or aggressively. Most of the time, I suffer from anxiety, depression, and low self-esteem. But the most troublesome of them all are the flashbacks. It's a never-ending struggle to get the thoughts out of my mind once they are there and it makes for a long day for everyone around me. Once I pray about it I'm able to fight through it, regain myself, and make sure the day is a productive one.

For many years, I opted out of family functions because I was afraid to see him. I've grown into a mature woman who is able to be at any event and see him and not flinch and want to kill him slowly anymore. However, he of course has to avoid any situation that would make him say a damn thing to me and we will be fine. There were times were it seemed like he wanted to say something, but I wouldn't stick around long enough to see; I avoided his eyes as much as he avoided mine, but there was no mistaking the fact that sometimes I would catch him gazing a little longer, his eyes lingering soulfully, but I could not stand the thought of it, the thoughts of him walking closer to me.

For years, I thought I wanted an apology from him, hell, I felt like I deserved one. It wasn't until 6 years ago that I realized that I could forgive him and my parents and be okay with not receiving an apology. That took a lot.

Many people cannot understand how I got to this place today, but when you I have lived as a prisoner of my thoughts for majority of your life, when you had no way out, nowhere to turn to, no one to talk to, you start seeing people and life for what it really is.

You start to get the deep distasteful message as to what life has to offer, it all begins to make sense to you, and you become your own teacher, your own role model, your own shoulder to lean on and your own best friend. You begin to understand the importance of controlling and being in charge of your life. I got this message delivered loud and clear in my heart, mind, and soul.

Hurdle: A hurdle, or an issue presented to a current situation that causes delays or prevents a process from developing is known as a setback.

Even the smallest setbacks are mostly unexpected and tend to be merciless. The duration of a current situation that is caused from a setback seem to last longer than we anticipate. In fact, this is the primary reason why they are called "setbacks" in the first place. Setbacks tend to 'set-you-back' in terms of emotional distress and psychological interruptions, leaving only utter trauma and pure turmoil in their wake.

The very worst thing about surviving a setback is that it effectively hurls you to 'ground zero'. To say that this is brutal would be a mild understatement.

Fortunately, as setbacks are evidently present in our past history, setbacks are also paradoxically a life game changer. The very nurseries that tend to germinate and eventually nurture all the comebacks are vividly present in such cases like diamonds. From an ugly, dull and black coal in high temperatures to gasses that seem to be stuck underground for a very, very longtime, gives birth to precious stones. As a matter of fact, most precious stones are usually placed in front of relatively dark backdrops in order to vividly enhance and bring out their beauty. "Therefore, I can simply say that from chaos, comes beauty..."

A Final Note

It took a long time for me to get over the loss of my mother. Not her physical body but the role a mother plays in a daughter's life. It's a special one. Not taking away fathers, but girls have babies and we set the blueprint for our children.

I craved and prayed for my mother for a long time and she never showed up—not in the way that I needed her too. I hurt myself a lot trying to build a relationship over the years but in all reality I lost my mother when I was fifteen and again at twenty-eight. For years, my mom and I had a strained relationship until I gained the ability to understand how to meet her where she was in her life.

As for my father, you didn't protect me like a father supposed too. You ignored all the signs. Your little girl was hurting and you did nothing, even when you found out you ignored my hurt me. All I can do is honor my father like the Bible says—nothing more or less.

I love my parents and it took me sometime to say that. I wouldn't trade them for the world. I forgive them. And for the man who abused me, I forgive him, and have risen above it all. I pray that God has mercy on him. To Stokley, Im sorry for taking advantage of you that day and I hope you can find a way to forgive me.

Despite the hardships, I have been blessed. All that mattered was finding peace and building myself to become a better version for myself. For a long time, I was so upset with God. I couldn't imagine how I was going through all of this and he not once helped me.

But he always did. Every time I needed him, he guided me to help that I didn't stick with. But that has changed.

I go to church, read the word more, and I started seeing a psychiatrist. I alternated between the psychiatrist and the psychologist for a while. I have grown stronger in my faith and started seeing positive things happening in my life. I no longer use alcohol or drugs. My addiction to reckless sexual behaviors is no longer on my mind. God will truly take away any addiction you have if you ask Him. As I continue to seek professional help it has allowed me to see how I came to make certain decisions and I how I had to get rid of all the things that I had chosen when I was a toxic person. Cleansing means something. Just as your home needs spring cleaning so does parts of your life.

Many things are starting to change and people are starting to fade away because I am starting to believe and walk in my faith and truth.

Regardless of my life's hurdles, God placed so many positive woman in my life. He gave me the wisdom to seek help in him through the people he placed in my path. That's what makes me blessed. God gave me a new heart and the ability to continue to fight through the pain because you will come out a winner no matter what.

"You have no cause for anything but gratitude and joy."—Guatama Budda

For a decade, I felt sorry for myself for what happened to me. I couldn't see how beautiful the sky was or know what it felt like to be free of things that held you down. Today, I have no business feeling anything other than joy and gratitude. In spite of it all, I managed to survive. I trusted God and believe that He had a plan for my life. So I live by giving and it brings my heart so much joy being able to put a smile on someone's face. I give people laughter and I spread love no matter where I am. When I say there is a good life after all of the bad things that could and did happen to you, trust me there is!

Let's start the movement. I laid the path and now let's walk this long road to recovery together. You will not be alone anymore, I promise.

SCRAPES AND SCARS
No Secrets

12-Day
JOURNAL

Scrapes and Scars: No Secrets is a journal of healing, empowerment and loving yourself. I am like you, a survivor of sexual abuse. For many years, I searched high and low for an understanding of why it happened to me and for the ability to live life afterward. I do not have the answers to all of your questions, however, we share the same pain. Over the years, I've found peace of mind by doing the things that I have listed in this journal. I hope that you find some of these steps helpful in your journey for peace of mind and healing. What I recommend to all of you is to seek professional help.

For the next 12 days, I will take you on a journey of healing by giving you some of the tools that helped me overcome my challenges. These steps cannot and will not be completed all at once, one or more you may have to go back and accomplish later. Pick a time and a quiet room in your place to sit down with me every day and just become a better you.

"When the mind is pure, joy follows like a shadow that never leaves"—Buddha

Day One

Healing: Making the decision to heal is very important. This is something that you have to want for yourself and no one else. So, are you ready to heal? If so, Why?

Q: Are you ready to heal? If so why now?
_____
_____
_____

Q: I'm proud of myself today because I…
_____
_____
_____

Q: This commitment to healing is important to me because…
_____
_____
_____

Q: What I love most about myself today is…
_____
_____
_____

Q: Music/Movie mood today is…
_____
_____
_____

"Life is not about waiting for the storm to pass, it's all about learning to dance in the rain"—Vivian Greene

Day Two

Why Me? Dealing with the memories that have been stored deep down inside needs to come out, it is not healthy for our bodies. This stage might be the hardest reliving what happened. Talk about it to yourself aloud.

Q: Why not you... If not you, then who...
_____
_____
_____

Q: I used to be afraid of...
_____
_____
_____

Q: I'm proud of myself today because I...
_____
_____
_____

Q: What I love most about myself today is...
_____
_____
_____

Q: Music/Movie mood today is...
_____
_____
_____

"Healing doesn't mean the damage never existed, it means the damage no longer controls our lives"—Akshay Dubey

Day Three

Feeling your scars? Remembering the feeling that you felt when it happened to you. Write down everything you feel? Close your eyes and get in touch with how you felt that day?

Q: I'm proud of myself today because I...
___
___
___

Q: What I learned about myself today was...
___
___
___

Q: What inspires you and why?
___
___
___

Q: What I love most about myself today is...
___
___
___

Q: Music/Movie mood is...
___
___
___

"Sometimes it's the smallest decision that can change your life forever"—*Keri Russell*

Day Four

Accepting the past: For me, I wanted to believe it didn't happen to me. Well then reality hit and I was faced with the traumas of what happened and it is never going away no matter how hard we try. But accepting that it happens to you and that it does not define you is important.

Q: What I learned about myself today was…

_____
_____
_____

Q: Thoughts after accepting the past…

_____
_____
_____

Q: Music/Movie mood…

_____
_____
_____

Q: What I love most about myself today is…

_____
_____
_____

"Grief is in two parts. The first is loss. The second is the remaking of life."—Anne Roiphe

Day Five

No more secrets. Grieve what's lost. Most women are embarrassed to talk about it because they may feel its their fault. Well, it's not. Talking about it brings you strength and power. Let's confide in someone and make him or her aware of what's been hurting us for so long.

Q: How does living with scars affect your everyday living?
___
___
___

Q: How do you feel about yourself today?
___
___
___

Q: I'm proud of myself today because…
___
___
___

Q: What I love most about myself today is…
___
___
___

Q: Music/Movie mood today…
___
___
___

"Not everything that is faced can be changed. But nothing can be changed until it is faced"—James Baldwin

Day Six

The Blame game. Many survivors blame themselves for what happened. They say things like: I should not have been there or I should not have worn that. Many people never blame the abuser for what he or she did. This is not your burden to carry, we did nothing wrong. Direct the blame to the abuser he or she did the unthinkable to you not the other way around. Understand that it was not your fault.

Q: Did you blame yourself for what happened? If so, list three reasons why.
_____
_____
_____

Q: Write three reasons why it is not your fault and say them five times each.
_____
_____
_____

Q: Did you ignore what happened in hopes that it would go away?
_____
_____
_____

Q: I'm proud of myself today because I…
_____
_____
_____

Q: What I love most about myself today is…
_____
_____
_____

"Self-compassion is nurturing yourself with all the kindness and love you would shower on someone else you cherish"—
Dr. Debra L. Reble

Day Seven

Embracing the child or woman you were when it happened. Feeling the compassion for yourself is important. It is okay to feel for yourself. It is a part of taking care of you.

Q: Before being violated I used to love or enjoy…
___
___
___

Q: What I learned about myself was…
___
___
___

Q: What I love most about myself today is…
___
___
___

Q: Music/movie mood today is…
___
___
___

"Work on being in love with the person in the mirror who has been through so much but is still standing"—Unknown

Day Eight

Learning to love yourself again. Treat yourself to a day that is filled with loving you?

Q: Write down what you did for yourself and why?
___
___
___

Q: How did you feel afterward or during your love yourself day?
___
___
___

Q: What I love most about myself today is…
___
___
___

Q: What I learned about myself today was…
___
___
___

Q: Music/Movie mood today is…
___
___
___

"Holding on to anger is like drinking poison and expecting the other person to die"—Buddha

Day Nine

Anger. It is a powerful emotion. Some survivors believe that being angry is a sign of weakness. However, it's a sign of being healthy. Directing anger towards the people who deserve it the most like the abuser, a family member who didn't protect you and whomever you feel deserves it. Don't cheat yourself of anger, it will cause more problems like depression, anxiety, and aggression. Express your anger to a friend, write a letter, scream it at the top of your lungs.

Q: In what ways did you express your anger?

_____
_____
_____

Q: How did you feel afterward…

_____
_____
_____

Q: what I learned about myself today was…

_____
_____
_____

Q: What I love most about myself today is…

_____
_____
_____

Q: Music/Movie mood today is…

_____
_____
_____

"For I will restore health to you and heal you of your wounds," says the Lord."—*Jeremiah 30:17*

Day Ten

Best Day is the Moment of truth. I call this the best day because when you are able to confront the person who hurt you whether in court, on the street, a meeting with family (if a family member) its empowering. However, this phase is not for everyone. I repeat this phase is not for everyone. No matter what they say if it is an apology, denial, sentencing day in court; it's the fact that you can say to them what he or she has done. It's meant in an attempt to sometimes close the chapter that remained open for so long in your life. This can be helpful.

Q: If you could face your abuser what would you say to him or her? If you did what happened?

_____
_____
_____

Q: what I learned about myself today was that I am...

_____
_____
_____

Q: what are your thoughts on today's moment of truth...

_____
_____
_____

Q: What I love most about myself today is...

_____
_____
_____

"I eventually come to understand that harboring the anger, the bitterness and resentment towards those that hurt me, I was giving the rein of control over to them. Forgiving was not about accepting their words and deeds. Forgiving was about letting go and moving on with my life. In doing so, I had finally set myself free"—Deerheart Wolf

Day Eleven

Forgiveness. You will never get over what has happened to you but cleansing your soul of all the feeling of hurt is important. Forgiving someone who hurt you is never for them, but for you. It is so that you are able to live your best life free and clear of bitterness, pain, resentment, and anger. Live for the present; get rid of the past, and let's look forward to our futures.

Q: What I love most about myself today is…

_____
_____
_____

Q: Are you living your truth…

_____
_____
_____

Q: What legacy you want to be remembered by…

_____
_____
_____

Q: How do you know you have forgiven everyone who hurt you…

_____
_____
_____

Q: Music/Movie mood today is…

_____
_____
_____

"I am not what happened to me, I am who I choose to become"—Carl Gustav Lung

Day Twelve

Who are you? After experiencing a childhood trauma like sexual abuse, I hid the little girl inside of me for years. I struggle with my own identity and lost sight of my hopes and dreams. Today is all you.

Q: If you did not experience the hurt of being abused would you be a different person?

_____
_____

Q: What are your biggest accomplishments to date?

_____
_____

Q: What motivates you?

_____
_____

Q: What I love most about who I am today is…

_____
_____

Q: I am really good at…

_____
_____

"Forgiveness is not an occasional act, it is a permanent attitude"—*Dr. Martin Luther King Jr.*

Now that we reached the end write down your own thoughts, goals, and strategies that can help someone else get through their struggles with sexual abuse...

_____
_____
_____
_____
_____
_____
_____
_____
_____
_____
_____
_____
_____
_____
_____
_____
_____
_____
_____
_____
_____
_____
_____
_____
_____
_____
_____
_____
_____
_____
_____
_____

www.ingramcontent.com/pod-product-compliance
Lightning Source LLC
Chambersburg PA
CBHW021153080526
44588CB00008B/321